# MOTHER OF MERCY

by
Lioné, Valé,
Levuté and Adelé

*All booklets are published thanks to the
generous support of the members of the
Catholic Truth Society*

CATHOLIC TRUTH SOCIETY
PUBLISHERS TO THE HOLY SEE

## CONTENTS

## PREFACE

I am very pleased to be asked to write a few words as the preface for this book of remarkable prayers.

Here you will find great nourishment for your spiritual life. These prayers were composed by four Lithuanian girls imprisoned in a Siberian labour camp. Their generosity of spirit and vision, which carried them far beyond their immediate experiences, can help to raise our spirits beyond our immediate surroundings, whatever they may be. In particular I was moved by the prayers that centre on the Sacrifice of the Mass. These girls cannot have had that many opportunities of being part of the celebration of Mass. Most of us can do so whenever we wish. These prayers can help us to enter more deeply into the meaning of the Mass and to know that in taking part in it we are praying for and with people all over the world.

I hope that all of us who use these prayers may be inspired to accept more generously the demands of our daily life and unite them with Christ in his offering of love to the father. In that way even our most burdensome moments can become a benefit to many whom we might never know or see.

+Vincent Nichols

Archbishop of Birmingham
6 November 2001

*Pranute,*
*kad galėtumėt geriau kartu su mumis jausti, mąstyti ir garbinti Viešpatį, siunčiame šią knygutę Lionė G. padarė ją, Valė ją ser. piešė, Levutė Vis. suklijavo, o aš rašiau.*

*1953. II. 16*     *Ad*

Frances,
We send this prayer book to you
in order that you may be able
better to feel, think, and
worship the Lord together
with us.
Lioné made it, Valé drew it,
Levuté glued it together,
and I wrote it.

16th February 1953, Ad(elé).

The photograph shows the original hand-written book of prayers, which measures 2 by 3 inches. It was composed in 1953 by four Lithuanian girls, deported to Siberia in the post-war purges. Having no prayer-book of their own, they resolved to write one for their own use. The book found its way to the West, and has been published in eight languages.

## MORNING AND EVENING PRAYERS

**O Heaven, Bless this day of toil.**

A day of hard toil is dawning.
Blessed Trinity,
I wish to glorify You
by patience and respect
for my fellow workers.
Give us wisdom and strength
to endure calmly
all misunderstanding,
contempt, and hatred.

Bless those dear to me,
my whole nation, and especially
the defenders of my country,
orphans, and all those
who suffer for the Truth.
Unite us all by lively faith,
unquenchable hope,
and love that knows no bounds. Amen.

Martyrs of our nation,
obtain wisdom, strength
and unity
for the labourers of our nation.
Obtain an endless,
bright repose for those
who have laid down their lives
for their native land. Amen.

My Guardian Angel,
My Patron, Saint Anthony,
and all blessed spirits,
protect, direct, and keep me free
from all evil today. Amen.

Holy Spirit,
enlighten both my own
and my nation's paths,
leading to a happy future.
Bless our resolutions. Amen.

Saint Teresa,
Patroness of the Missions,
obtain for us apostolic ardour,
help us, by our good example,
to harvest many souls
for our Lord. Amen.

## O Lord, Bless my Sleep

The day has closed its eyes.
Fatigue closes my eyes.
My feelings have dried up,
my strength has left me.
O Lord, I thank You
for all Your graces of today:
for health, strength, and food,
both that of soul and of body;
for every kind word,
for every pleasant thing;
for hope, for my native tongue
that I hear
in this strange country.
I thank You for the suffering,
the hatred, and all the crosses
whereby You tested me.
Lord, I beg of You
peaceful rest for myself
and my dear ones. Amen.

Holy Family,
protect and foster
the peace of our home,
and our yearning
for the Truth; shield from evil
the edifice of our nation,

and let us,
the children of sorrow,
spend some time,
at least in our dreams,
with our dear ones
left in our country. Amen.

Mary,
I appeal to your mercy.
Comforter of the afflicted,
console the children
of a land sprinkled
with blood and tears.
Console the banished
and comfort our hearts
filled with suffering,
sorrow, and homesickness.

Mary, I entreat your help
for the defenders
of our country.

I beg of you calm repose
for those who laid down
their lives for their native land.
I ask of you lasting peace
for my dear country and
for the entire exhausted world.

Mary, I raise
my weary hands to you,
pleading that you pray to God
for forgiveness of faults, sins,
misdeeds, and imperfections;
both mine and
those of my dear ones. Amen.

All for Jesus, day and night!

## THE SACRIFICE OF THE MASS

### Introit

O Lord, at this very moment
a priest is bowing
before Your altar
on behalf of all the world
and on my behalf.

Lord,
forgive me my transgressions
and strengthen me
that I may accomplish
my duties perfectly.
Together with
Your tremendous sacrifice
and the merits of the saints,
placed in the treasury
of the Church,
accept my suffering
and fatigue, humiliations,
tears of longing,
hunger and cold,
all my soul's infirmities,
all my efforts for the freedom

# Šv. Mišių
# Auka

Įžanga.

Ir šioje valan-
doje kunigas lenkia-
si prieš Tavo altorių,
Viešpatie, né ang pa-
saulį, taip pat ir
už mane. Viešpatie

Reproduction of a page in the prayer book: the Sacrifice of the Mass.

of my country, for the welfare
of my friends and my dear ones,
for the souls of those
who fought and died.
O Lord, have mercy on those
who persecute and torment us;
grant to them also the grace
to know
the sweetness of Your love.


**Blessed Trinity, have mercy!**

O heavenly Father,
You have created us
for perfect happiness.
In all humility I pray,
lead me to it, as You please,
down steep cliffs
and through bitter cold.
Everywhere I will follow You;
only show me the way.
O Lord Jesus,
You have sacrificed
everything for our salvation.
In order to teach us,
You have drained to the dregs
life's bitter chalice.

You have chosen for me
the same road of suffering,
the lot of destitution
and homesickness.
Strengthen me for these.
Holy Spirit,
enlighten me in the hour
of darkness and temptation,
that I may neither go astray
nor live in deadly error.

### The Holy Gospel

O Lord, grant me the grace
to understand
Your teaching more and more.
Give me the wisdom
to profess it everywhere
and to proclaim it by my deeds.
Allow me so to love it
that every day and everywhere
I shall make known
the greatness
of Your mercy and love.

## Offertory

O Lord,
because of Your greatest love,
You descended from heaven
and walked the paths
of this earth doing good.

You endured
most painful sufferings
in soul and in body.
You have chosen me
to walk the road of the elect.

I wish to follow You, O Lord,
only lead me,
give me strength and wisdom,
and brighten my desires.

With a grateful heart,
I will accept everything
from Your hands:
helplessness, endless longing,
contempt, neglect
and disregard, the loss
of those dearest to me
and of my liberty.

Lord, do with me
whatever You desire;
only have compassion
on my nation
and on my beloved ones.


### Canon and Consecration

O Lord, You listen
to the cry of every priest
and descend from heaven
upon our altars.

Bread and wine, by Your desire,
become Your most sacred
Body and Blood.
In Your divinity You come
to strengthen,
to console and comfort us.

I beg of You, dear Saviour,
change my whole being:
make of me, who am selfishly
concerned about myself
and drowned
in daily drudgery,
one who is considerate

and helpful to others.
Make me understand
their cares and troubles,
lest I judge them rashly.
Transform my countenance
and that of my dear country.
Raise us up that every one of us
may seek the way to You,
that we may count no sacrifice
too great
for Your love and glory.


## Holy Communion

When my soul weeps,
when my heart
is full of longing,
when my whole being shivers
with fatigue, come, O Jesus,
I beg You to come.
Draw near to revive
and console me.
What is it
You wish to tell me
by means of these people,
in these surroundings,
by this span of time?

Jesus,
I implore You to shorten
the time of trial for us,
for my dear ones,
for my exhausted nation.

Jesus, I ask You, help those
who laid down their lives
for our welfare;
assist them for whom
You wish me to pray.

### The End of Mass

O Saviour, through Your
most holy sacrifice,
through the offerings
and prayers
of those close to me,
through those
who have suffered
and laid down their lives
for my dear country,
and through the merits
of all the saints in heaven,
strengthen me in my toil today
and for my duties tomorrow.
Amen.

## Mary, Save Us

Mary, save the land
woven with blood and tears,
with self-sacrifice,
resolutions and love.

Mary, awaken in our breasts
the strength of giants.
Preserve the pure spirit
of our nation,
cherished by our forefathers
through the ages.

Mary, enlighten those
who have wandered astray,
intercede for the souls
of the freedom-fighters.
Raise up our holy Lithuania
that it may radiate and shine
like a splendid star
to glorify you and your Son's
boundless mercy and love.
Amen.

## PRAYERS FOR CONFESSION AND HOLY COMMUNION

### Before the Examination of Conscience

Lord, I have sought happiness
everywhere and always,
but my heart can find
neither rest nor peace.

Jesus, true joy and happiness
are to be found only in You.
Cast only one glance at me
and all storms will cease in me.

I will seek only You
and will proclaim Your mercy.

Holy Spirit,
enlighten my mind;
show me the way
to eternal bliss.
To reach it I will spare nothing,
I will sacrifice everything.
Holy Virgin and all Heaven,
help me
to keep my resolutions.

### Examination of Conscience

In regard to God:
Do I see
God's will in everything?
Do I realise
that the way of suffering
is destined for me?
Is despair destroying me?
In regard to my neighbour:
Do I do any harm
to my neighbour?
Do I distrust,
defame or deride,
denounce or despise?
Do I lay on others
my own burdens,
my own work or bad mood?
What about fear of criticism;
or lying, contempt, revenge,
curbing the freedom of others,
or thoughtlessness in speech?
In regard to myself:
Do I desire sickness?
Do I harm my own health?
Was I unchaste, egocentric?

### An Act of Contrition

Saviour, I have cast away
Your Passion, love, and desires.
I have condemned myself
and become
profoundly unhappy.
With all my being,
I implore You:
cast Your glance at me,
cover up my transgressions,
raise me up that with joy
I may hasten to You
to worship Your mercy
and ineffable love. Amen.


### Prayers before Holy Communion

Draw near, all holy angels;
draw near,
all saints of heaven,
Immaculate Mother,
Saint Joseph, Saint Teresa,
come to praise
the Lord of Mercy,
the God of Love.
Teach me how to be humble,
how to love,

that everywhere and always
I may live in gratitude
and with my entire life
I may proclaim
God's love and goodness.

## Prayers after Holy Communion

Jesus, You have come to me.
Remain with me forever.
Live in me. Teach me,
painful though it be.
Rest in me,
and never forsake me.
With all my being,
to You I cling,
praising and thanking You
for coming,
for Your consolation,
for all the other graces
You have brought
to me and to my home.

O Heart of Jesus,
burning with love,
have mercy on those
who fight for freedom,
who have died on the battlefield

or still are suffering
for my country.

Have mercy on all
in whose stead
I should pray and praise You.
O God of Mercy,
I thank You for the hearts
who have done me
so much good
and who never forget me.

I thank You also for those
who, by their hatred,
teach and warn me. Amen.

### Prayer for Parents

Mary, Advocate of Sinners,
Comforter of the Afflicted,
Mother of Mercy,
with my heart full of sorrow,
I implore your help
for my departed parents,
who guarded and protected
our family on earth
by their care and toil.
Mary, obtain for them

the grace to be united
to your Son without delay
that they from above
may guide us again
and lead us out of the pitfalls,
temptations, snares,
and storms of this life. Amen.

## LET US MEDITATE ON THE PASSION OF OUR LORD JESUS CHRIST

### Introduction

O Jesus, who walked
the royal road of suffering,
Queen of Martyrs,
and all you martyrs
on earth and in heaven,
help me
to understand the meaning
of our Saviour's love
and suffering.

Help me and those dear to me
and our whole nation
to discover our way.

### 1. Jesus is Condemned to Die

"Judge not,
that you may not be judged".

I judge and condemn,
I sneer and deride,
I become angry and curse,

I nurture revenge
and reveal faults
and secrets of others.

Let us improve everything,
but only by goodness.
Love is the best teacher.
No hurdles can obstruct its way.

"There is no greater love
than this, that a man lay down
his life for his friends."

**Prayer**

Jesus, have mercy
on those who condemn;
have mercy on unjust judges.
Protect us from meddling
in the affairs of others.

## 2. Jesus takes His Cross

God has forgotten me.
He does not answer my prayers.
Why do I suffer?
I did not steal.
I did not kill.
Why so many hardships for me?

Hunger and cold,
throbbing pains in my bones,
contempt and rude blows,
discomfort and neglect.
"O all you
that pass by the way,
stop and see if there be
any sorrow like to mine".

### Prayer

Jesus, what do You wish
to tell me by this pain?
In everything that happens
let me fully understand
all You want of me.
"Behold, I am
the handmaid of the Lord."

## 3. Jesus falls under the Cross for the First Time

A habit is a second nature.
Let us help
children and the young
by our good example,
by gentle counsel
and vigilant protection.
Thus, let us dispel
the plight that fosters evil.

**Prayer**

Jesus, protect our youth
from a first fall.
Help those who have fallen
to rise again.
Grant me the spirit to radiate
Your love and goodness.

### 4. Jesus meets His Mother

Two glowing torchlights -
the sun and the moon -
the most beloved Son
and the most noble Mother
meet on the street of salvation.
Two hearts taste all bitterness
of suffering and of sorrow.
Two hearts - most sensitive
to our own troubles and misery.

**Prayer**

O sorrowful Mother, aid me
to understand the meaning
of present hardships.
Help us all
to return soon
to our beloved land
and to find the way
to everlasting happiness.

## 5. Simon of Cyrene helps Jesus to carry His Cross

When I visit the sick,
when I console the downcast,
when I pray for the departed
and for those in error,
when I assist the widows,
the old, and the orphans,
when I radiate God by my life,
then - even today -
I help Jesus carry His cross.

### Prayer

Holy Spirit,
give me knowledge,
wisdom, and strength
to do good,
to become more holy,
and to glorify
my Saviour's Passion.
Holy Spirit,
let me daily recognise
the thoughts given by God.

## 6. Veronica wipes the Face of Jesus

Let us paint
a picture of Jesus in our hearts,
while we fight for truth,
for goodness, and for beauty.

**Prayer**

Jesus, help me
to understand correctly
the values of truth,
goodness and beauty.
Let me strive for them
unceasingly,
that I may serve God
and my homeland
with my whole being.

### 7. Jesus falls the Second Time

Let us avoid
impure thoughts and feelings.
Let us foster and cherish
the virtue of chastity.
Let us assist our young people
by an exemplary life.

**Prayer**

Jesus, who loves purity,
instill undying ideals of purity
in the children of Mary's land,
the land of green rue,
of lilies and tulips.

## 8. Jesus consoles the Weeping Women

To have compassion
for the suffering of Jesus
means assisting the sick,
helping the forlorn and those
who suffer anguish in soul
and in body.

### Prayer

Jesus, who did console
the women of Jerusalem,
console today,
with Your precious Passion,
our sisters, daughters,
brides, wives and mothers,
who are oppressed by sorrow.

## 9. Jesus falls the Third Time

Utter despair,
boundless anguish of soul,
crushing fatigue of body,
and the powerlessness
of old age,
these are what pinion
the wings that would soar
in spiritual flights.

**Prayer**

Jesus, who was weary
and exhausted,
help me and those dear to me
to endure patiently
the helpless weakness
of our souls and bodies.

## 10. Jesus is Stripped of His Garments

Ignominy of our bodies,
nakedness of our souls,
total destitution -
this is the way
we are stripped.

**Prayer**

Jesus, protect us
from extreme poverty
that leads to crime
and impedes
the progress of the soul.

## 11. Jesus is Nailed to the Cross

By what,
if not by our offences,
our anger, bad moods,
hatred and revenge
do we murder other souls?

**Prayer**

Jesus, teach me
not to infringe
on the liberty of others.
Grant me forbearance
to endure all anguish,
sorrow, scorn, neglect,
and, if need be,
bitter death itself;
but do not punish
either me or my nation
by everlasting damnation.

## 12. Jesus Dies on the Cross

"I have nothing in this world",
says Christ.
The spirit of this world
is pride and self-love,
vainglory, greed, and jealousy.

**Prayer**

Saviour, help me to die
to the spirit of this world
and to feel joy in living
humbly and generously,
purely and prayerfully.

### 13. Jesus is taken down from the Cross

Let us not thrust aside
the hand
that is outstretched to us.

### Prayer

Saviour, I entreat Your help
for my departed friends.
I beseech Your consolation
for those saddened by the death
of their beloved ones.
I beg You to hear
the supplications
of those crying to You.

### 14. Jesus is Laid in the Tomb

### Prayer

Jesus, help those
who die in foreign lands
without the consolation
of the Church
or their dear ones,
without the comfort and aid
of their friends.

## The End of the Way

Jesus, through the merits
of Your Passion,
through the sacrifices
of the Queen of Martyrs,
and of all the martyrs,
through my own
and my nation's desires,
cover up my own
and my nation's transgressions
and help us all
to find the way to You,
that we may not die
in misery or want,
in hunger or despair.
Jesus, deliver the world
from going down to perdition.
Amen.

Pray for the intentions
of the Holy Father.

## PRAYERS ON FEASTS AND TO THE SAINTS

### Christmas Prayer

With icy lips,
with tearful cries,
tormented by despair, we fly
to Your straw-covered crib,
O Holy Babe!

Accept our petitions
and prayers,
Accept our longing
and resolves.

Accept the sacrifices
of our freedom-fighters.
Accept the tears
of our loved ones,
their sighs, their grief
and their anxieties.

Preserve us all
for a blessed future.
Grant heavenly bliss
to those who have died

from hunger and hardship
in foreign lands.

Through the merits
of Your Holy Mother
and of all the saints,
have pity on my dear ones
and on my whole nation.

With a bruised heart,
I implore You -
cut short the days of our trials.

If You wish a sacrifice,
take it from me,
but give me
the courage and fortitude
of the martyrs. Amen.

### Easter Prayer

O God, ineffable Love,
You Yourself have descended
from heaven to show us the way
to the kingdom of love.
Jesus, You have called
to eternal bliss
all men of good will,

all those who seek
and search for eternity.
Suffering of body and of soul
and want for everything
are the safest escort
to heavenly bliss.

Christ of the Resurrection,
raise me up from my faults.
Uplift my dear ones,
my nation, and also those
who have gone astray.
All celestial spirits,
aid us in singing the glory
of Christ's resurrection.

Glory, honour,
and thanksgiving
to the Conqueror of Death,
to the Giver of Love! Amen.

### Prayer to the Merciful Jesus

(Low Sunday)

Fatigue and weakness
fetter our hearts.
We have no food for our souls,

nor the rest that we need,
nor any refreshment.
Homesickness, nostalgia,
slavery have overwhelmed us.
O compassionate Jesus,
we call upon Your mercy.

We cleave
to Your transfixed side.
Most merciful Heart,
inflamed by love, unite us
with the bonds of mercy,
of love and unanimity.

Allow us
to return without delay
to our native land
that we may ever
better fulfil the duties
You have assigned to us.
Amen.

### Ascension Prayer

Jesus, You have revealed to us
an infinite secret of the soul;
mercy without limit,
all-conquering love,

the power
that springs from humility;
You manifested
suffering and sorrow
as a healing balm for the soul.
Jesus, led by angels,
Seraphim and Cherubim,
You ascended to heaven
for the jubilation of the saints.
Yet for us You have remained
throughout all days
in the Sacrament of Love.
Jesus, source of all bliss,
allow us to enjoy this life
as a gift of God,
but protect us
from attaching ourselves
merely to what this earth
can offer us.
Teach us to seek and to strive
for heaven's treasures. Amen.

## Pentecost Prayer

Waiting
for the promised Paraclete,
the apostles prayed ardently
together with Jesus' Mother.

The day of Pentecost came
and flames of fire
descended upon them,
enlightening them
and bringing them
apostolic fervour,
the courage of martyrs,
wisdom,
and the gift of tongues.

Come, Holy Spirit,
Comforter and Confirmer,
come down upon us.
We are waiting for You;
we are asking for You;
we are praying to You.

Come and renew us,
come and revive our nation.

Bring us
all the graces we need
that, united by love
we may establish
God's kingdom
in our homeland. Amen.

## Corpus Christi Prayer

I am in need of a physician.
I am in need of a consoler.
I am in need of a Father,
the best of all fathers.

Jesus, my Lord,
You have remained with us
through all the days
in the Sacrament of Love.
You call,
You appeal to all
who are saddened
and weary at heart.
Longing, I yearn,
yearning, I desire
to be united with You
in the Sacrament of Love.
Jesus, my Lord,
come to me,
comfort me, console me.
Visit the hearts
yearning for You
in strange lands.
Visit the dying and those
who have died without You.

Jesus, my Lord,
visit also those
who persecute You.

Lord Jesus, You are my light
in the darkness.
You are my warmth
in the cold.
You are my happiness
in sorrow.

The sun at daytime calls me
to come to You.
The twinkling stars at midnight
beckon me to fly to You.
Snow and white blossoms
speak to me of Your purity,
O Lord. Amen.

### Prayer to the Mother of Mercy at Girkalnis
(8 February 1943)

We have gone astray.
We are weary and cold.
Mother of Mercy, once again
you have not left us alone
in the days
of sorrow and affliction.

Again from heaven
you descended
in the brightness
of refulgent light
to visit our bloodstained land.
Mother, to whom -
to whom shall we flee,
to whom shall we appeal
in loneliness,
affliction, and distress?
Cast your glance, O Mother,
at our hearts, bruised
by sorrow and longing;
at our lips,
blue from hunger and cold.
Bring us back to the land
that heaven itself
has given us; to the land
adorned with churches
and wayside crosses;
to the land you have loved
from the very beginning.
Allow us to see again
the pictures and shrines
abounding in grace.
Permit us
to sing again the hymns

of gratitude and love
to the merciful Jesus
and to you, O Mother of Pity,
to you who have promised
to obtain the remission
of all transgressions. Amen.

### Prayer to St Casimir

Saint Casimir,
Patron of Mary's land,
who did honour
the Blessed Virgin with hymns;
who, while kneeling at night
at the door of the church,
did pray for her aid;
you loved purity so dearly
that for it you even forsook
all earthly comforts
and honour.

Our holy Patron,
obtain for our land
the flowers of purity
that by their sweet smell
they may draw us
to your ways.
Saint Casimir,

you were unwilling to leave
your land,
and when it was in danger,
you aided our armies.
With aching hearts, we beg you:
help our country
to rise again to noble life.

Help us
to return without delay
to our land consecrated
by the blood of martyrs,
by innocent tears
and boundless anguish.
Amen.

## Prayer to St Joseph

Saint Joseph,
Protector of the Holy Family,
assist
our newly-wedded families,
that the torches of love,
once kindled,
may never die out in them,
but that they may become
beacons that no winds
can extinguish.

Bring us back to
our family homes
for great creative work.
Saint Joseph,
you yourself have undergone
the lot of exile.

Obtain for us, weary ones,
wisdom and endurance,
lest we collapse
during the days of affliction,
that all hardships
may strengthen us
as fire strengthens steel.

Saint Joseph,
you are the steward
of all spiritual treasures.
Give us
the spirit of purity, of love,
fortitude and unity. Amen.

### Prayer to St Monica
(4 May)

Saint Monica,
you had to endure
the sinful errors

of your husband and your son.
Yet you brought them back
to the path of truth
by unwavering prayer,
sacrifice, and
the ardent spirit of penance,
in which you persisted
for many years.

Help our families to uproot
the weeds of vice,
especially drunkenness,
broken vows,
contempt of faith,
sins against chastity.
Obtain for us perseverance,
trust in God,
and the spirit of true penance.

Saint Augustine,
you who walked in error
for so long, obtain
for those now in error
the grace to know the truth.
Protect from error and crime
our young people
who are being misled

by their teachers
and weakened
by their bad example.

Mother Mary,
with heartfelt cries
of piercing anguish,
we implore your help.
Obtain for us
the strength and endurance
of Monica's spirit.
Amen.

### Prayer to the Mediatrix of All Graces
(24 May)

We are drained of strength;
our feelings have faded away;
our hearts are benumbed;
our thoughts
we cannot control.

Mary, full of grace,
Mediatrix of all Graces,
with contrite hearts,
we raise our suppliant hands.
Refresh us; tell us
what your beloved Son

wants of us.
We desire to surrender
wholly to His will.

Most gracious Virgin,
show us the stars - of faith,
lively in the newness
of its splendour;
of hope that is immortal;
of love that knows no bounds.

Help me and my nation
to overcome all obstacles
that impede our journey
to your Son's
embracing hands,
to His Heart
in wealth abounding. Amen.

### Prayer to St Anthony

Saint Anthony,
conqueror of all error
and of all slavery,
from the depths of our hearts
in these difficult days
we cry to you for help.

We have lost
a precious pearl of pearls -

our freedom.
We implore you -
recover it for us and teach us
to cherish, to love
and to defend it.

Help us to overcome
the slavery in ourselves;
to banish from our midst
flattery and accusations,
hatred and revenge,
interference
with the affairs of others,
that I may not destroy
the liberty of others.

Saint Anthony,
help me and my nation
to rise from negligence and error
to a brighter future.
Amen.

### Prayer to St John the Baptist

Saint John the Baptist,
who did cry out
to make the roads straight
for the Saviour,

help me and those dear to me
to straighten for Him
the paths of our hearts.

Teach us
by our life
to glorify Him,
to confess Him,
to love Him.

Help my nation
to understand His teaching,
to proclaim it,
and to live by it. Amen.

### Prayer to St Aloysius

Saint Aloysius,
who, in your whole life,
did blossom
as a white flower,
breathing fresh air,
radiating inner gladness;
who did grow in the sunlight,
blossom and bear fruit;
aid us from above.

Help our nation's searchers
to find inner life.

Escort us all
along the paths
of noble ideals. Amen.

### Prayer to Christ the King

Christ our King,
You have descended
from the throne of the cross
to reign in tender hearts.
From the throne of the cross
You have shown
to mankind
the road to the land of bliss.
On the throne of the cross
You have opened to us
the marvellous wealth
of Your Heart.

O King of Souls, I thank You
for letting me grow
in the shadow of the cross.

Saviour, allow me,
my dear ones, and my nation,
to feel the warmth, and love,
and strength of Your Heart.
Amen.

## All the Saints, Help Us

Angelic infants,
innocent virgins,
militant youths and confessors,
seekers of truth,
its lovers and heralds,
martyrs and sufferers,
help us to obtain
the all-colourful blossoms
of virtue.
Awaken in us
a yearning for God.

Patron saints
and martyrs of Lithuania,
we implore your aid
in our struggle
and endeavours. Amen.

## AID TO THE CHURCH IN NEED

This book is co-published with the Catholic charity **Aid to the Church in Need**, founded by the Dutch Norbertine Father Werenfried van Straaten. The charity helps the Church in need throughout the world, relieving the suffering of oppressed and persecuted Christians.

**Aid to the Church in Need** is involved in thousands of projects throughout the world: refugees are helped, churches rebuilt, seminarians trained, Bibles printed, priests and religious supported and the faith broadcast to the spiritually hungry.

Our only assets are the promises we make to poor and persecuted believers. You can help us to keep these promises by your donation, covenant or legacy. The National Director will be happy to provide any further information.

**Aid to the Church in Need** is a Public Association of the Catholic Church, directly dependent on the Holy See, providing pastoral relief throughout the world.

> Aid to the Church in Need
> 1 Times Square,
> Sutton, Surrey
> SM1 1LF
> Telephone: 020 8642 8668
> email: acn@acnuk.org
> website: www.acnuk.org

# Informative Catholic Reading

We hope that you have enjoyed reading this booklet.

If you would like to find out more about CTS booklets - we'll send you our free information pack and catalogue.

Please send us your details:

Name ..............................................................

Address ..........................................................

.........................................................................

.........................................................................

Postcode ........................................................

Telephone.......................................................

Email ..............................................................

Send to:    CTS, 40-46 Harleyford Road,
                Vauxhall, London
                SE11 5AY

Tel:  020 7640 0042
Fax: 020 7640 0046
Email: info@cts-online.org.uk

# Bring the riches of the faith to your parish community

Add a CTS dimension to your parish with our new bookstands

- Wall-mountable unit
- Free-standing unit
- Two-tier unit (wall-mountable or table-top)

Please send me information on CTS display units and the half price offer on books.